PIERRE OMIDYAR

THE FOUNDER OF ebaY®

INTERNET CAREER BIOGRAPHIES™

Pierre Omidyar

THE FOUNDER OF eBay®

JENNIFER VIEGAS

The Rosen Publishing Group, Inc., New York

To Anne Papineau Abboud, Norma Tanega, and Anthony Hardman, with whom I have enjoyed fond memories, and even a few laughs, about favorite items sold on eBay.

Published in 2007 by The Rosen Publishing Group, Inc.
29 East 21st Street, New York, NY 10010

First Edition

Library of Congress Cataloging-in-Publication Data

Viegas, Jennifer.
Pierre Omidyar: the founder of eBay/
Jennifer Viegas.—1st ed.
    p. cm.—(Internet career biographies)
Includes bibliographical references and index.
ISBN 1-4042-0715-5 (library binding)
1. Omidyar, Pierre, 1967-—Juvenile literature.
2. Executives—United States—Biography—Juvenile literature. 3. eBay (Firm)—Juvenile literature. 4. Internet auctions—Juvenile literature.
I. Title. II. Series.
HC102.5.O48V54 2007
381'.177092—dc22

                                                2005028804

Printed in China

On the cover: Pierre Omidyar stands tall and proud in front of a page from the eBay Web site, which he created.

CONTENTS

INTRODUCTION

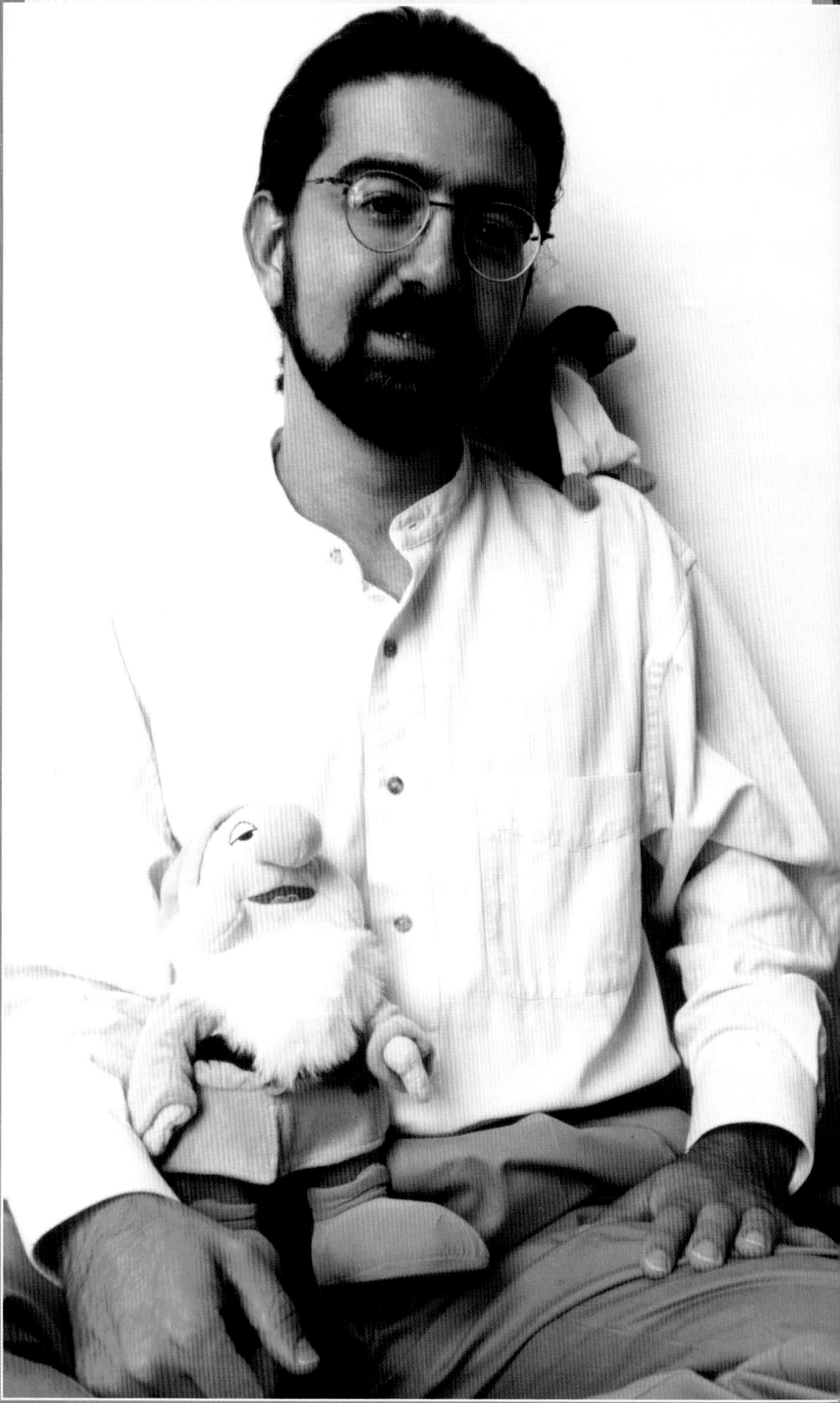

I n September of 1995, an unassuming little
advertisement was posted on Usenet, an uncen-
sored online newsgroup on what was then the
fledgling Internet. The ad, which was for an
online auction service called AuctionWeb, read:

AuctionWeb

"'The most fun buying and selling on the Web!'

- Run your own auction
- Bid on existing auctions
- New listings added daily!
- Fast, fun and FREE!
- AuctionWeb doesn't sell anything—we just
  provide the service. Try it out!"[1]

Not long after, a second announcement
appeared on the "What's New" page of the Web
site for the National Center for Supercomputing
Applications. The wording mirrored that of the
Usenet message: "The most fun buying and selling on the Web. Run an auction or join the fun
of an existing auction."[2]

AuctionWeb did not initially generate a lot
of interest. The site attracted zero visitors on its

Not many billionaire executives agree to be photographed holding stuffed toys, but Pierre Omidyar, founder of eBay, is not the
average businessperson. The eBay Web site has sold millions of
dollars worth of toys, including the popular Beanie Babies, over
the past decade.

first day of operation, which was Labor Day of 1995. This lack of interest was understandable, though, since people were out celebrating the long holiday weekend. Within a few months, however, news about the AuctionWeb site did spread. At first, only a handful of curious onlookers took a peek at the site's main page. Those few people probably liked what they saw and told their friends and families about it. Then even more visitors likely shared the link with others. Before long, the auction site had a loyal following.

Some computer users who saw the ad and passed up the invitation likely questioned how shopping on the Internet could be "fun," as it was described. "Convenient" probably came to mind as a more appropriate description. Amazon.com, then exclusively an online bookstore, was also in its infancy at that time. Most online shopping sites were just virtual storefronts for large, well-known retailers with brick-and-mortar, or physical, stores. The selection of items for sale in these storefronts seemed limited compared to the wide array of goods available in the brick-and-mortar stores themselves. Purchase methods on the sites were often awkward and seemingly not as safe against fraud as handing cash or a credit card over to a visible clerk. Customers paying by check usually had to fill out a form online and then send payment through postal mail, and many sites were not yet encrypted to protect customers paying with credit cards. Buying items on the Internet was still an untested business, but people were eager to experience the speed and ease of virtual shopping.

AuctionWeb, however, did not have a big, established name as did some of the brick-and-mortar stores that sold goods on the Internet. It was started by a young computer programmer named Pierre Omidyar. Although Omidyar was known by computer experts who frequented Usenet groups, his was not a household name. This is understandable, though, since he had not yet transformed AuctionWeb into the Internet auction behemoth that is now known as eBay. What is perhaps more astonishing is that a decade after AuctionWeb made its amazing transformation from a humble site to eBay, much remains unknown about Pierre Omidyar.

Chances are that you are not only familiar with eBay, but that you have also bought or sold something on the site. If you have participated in an eBay auction, then you are a member of the eBay community. The novelty of online auctions in the 1990s could explain eBay's success, but the originality of Omidyar's creation is only part of the story. The success of every business is determined by where it is and when it is introduced to the market.

AuctionWeb began in an area of Northern California nicknamed Silicon Valley. The name

Silicon Valley, shown here, was the hotbed for Internet start-ups in the late 1990s. In addition to eBay, technology companies such as Apple Computer and technology investment firms like Kleiner, Perkins, Caufield & Byers made their debuts here.

comes from the high-purity silicon used to make semiconductors, which are devices that affect the conductivity, or movement, of electricity. The control of electricity by use of semiconductors formed the basis of modern computing and the Internet. Omidyar lived and worked in Silicon Valley, along with other computer experts, so he was at the center of the Internet universe when he launched his online auction business.

The timing of AuctionWeb's introduction to the world was also perfect. Interest in online auctions had already started to grow in the early 1990s. More and more people were gaining access to the Internet. Thirty-seven million people aged sixteen and older in Canada and the United States had access to the Internet in 1995.[3] Just one year before, only six million people had access to the Internet. That means over six times the number of users in 1994 were surfing the Internet in 1995.[4] The astonishing increase was due to technological advances that allowed for home computers to be more reasonably priced and connected to the Internet. Suddenly personal computers were a must-have item for those who could afford them.

Was eBay's remarkable success the result of
luck or genius? Whichever it was, this business
tale has a very successful conclusion. Today, eBay
boasts millions of users. Pierre Omidyar became,

Meg Whitman, shown here with Omidyar, has every reason to
smile. Since she became president and CEO of eBay in March
1998, the company has become one of the leading Internet
commerce sites. Whitman worked at other companies before
eBay, such as FTD Flowers, which she led to great success just
as she has done with eBay.

and remains, one of the world's richest and most financially successful people. In 2005, his net worth was valued at approximately $10 billion.[5] *Forbes* magazine, which actually values Omidyar's wealth at the slightly higher figure of $10.2 billion, listed him as the eighteenth-richest person in America that same year.[6]

Who is Pierre Omidyar and how did he achieve such overwhelming success? He chose not to participate in this book project because, according to his spokesperson Michelle Goguen, he does not wish to authorize his biography at this point. That is understandable since Omidyar is still young and vibrant, with many adventures and goals that will undoubtedly fill more chapters of a future book. For now, though, let us go back in time to well before that fateful AuctionWeb start-up date in 1995 to learn how a person who had to overcome many obstacles built the worldwide business phenomenon we now know as eBay.

CHAPTER ONE

OMIDYAR'S EARLY YEARS

P ierre Omidyar was born on June 21, 1967, in Paris, France. He was given the name of Parviz by his Iranian parents.[1] Omidyar's grandparents on both sides of his family had sent their children to Paris to obtain quality educations that, in the early 1960s, were not available to most students in Iran.[2]

France has had a large Muslim population for many decades. Today, the eight million Muslims living in France constitute the largest Muslim population in Europe.[3] Most of these individuals come

As a young boy, Omidyar lived in Paris, shown here. The city greatly influenced his outlook on life. In 2004, Omidyar told *Esquire* magazine that when he was younger, he could remember philoso-phizing about each person in the busy city having his or her own path in life. Omidyar would soon realize his own track in life.

from nearby North Africa, so Muslims from other areas have formed tightly knit, smaller communities within the larger community. Though it is not known what religion Omidyar follows, it was through such a close community that Omidyar's mother, Elahé Mir-Djalali, and father, whose name remains undisclosed, met and married. Pierre was their only child.

ELAHÉ MIR-DJALALI OMIDYAR

Elahé Mir-Djalali Omidyar is well known in her own right as the founder and president of the Roshan Cultural Heritage Institute. The institute is a nonprofit organization that promotes and supports Persian culture (Persia is now Iran). Elahé Mir-Djalali Omidyar specializes in both linguistic and Persian studies.[4] She has taught at such prestigious universities as the University of California at Berkeley and Georgetown University. During her time in France she received a doctoral degree in linguistics with honors from the prestigious Université de la Sorbonne in France. She also earned two other master's degrees from Sorbonne and Georgetown.

Her field of expertise is linguistics, the study of languages. To better understand where Omidyar inherited his talents from, all language

THE INTERNET

Often called simply the Net, the Internet is a network of countless computers around the globe. Two basic types of computers allow for the operation of the Net. The first is a user computer, which is probably the kind you have if you own a computer. User computers enable people to access the Net. The second type is a Web server. This is a specially designed computer that can store Web pages and their information. If you create your own Web site, you will have to use a server to post the site to the Web. Servers charge a fee for this service, but without them, your Web site could only be viewed on your own computer and perhaps your home's individual computer network. The Internet allows sites, from simple personal Web pages to giant corporate sites such as eBay, to be viewed by anyone with access to a user computer.

works like code that represents certain ideas and thoughts. Different countries and cultures obviously have different languages, or ways of expressing the same, or similar, tangible and intangible things. In an interesting link between Elahé Mir-Djalali Omidyar's linguistic skills and her son's Internet savvy, computers function by code just as language does. When a programmer wants to make a computer perform a specific task, he or she writes code in a computer language structured to suit the device. Omidyar became fluent in computer languages at a young age, so while he did not go into the field of linguistics as his mother did, her work and academic achievements must have exerted an enormous influence on him.

OMIDYAR'S FATHER

Very little information about Omidyar's father has been released to the media. It is known that he studied science and worked as a urologist at Johns Hopkins University in Baltimore, Maryland. In fact, the entire Omidyar family emigrated from France to the United States because Omidyar's father accepted a residency at Johns Hopkins.

Omidyar's parents separated when he was just a young boy, but he indicated that his father was always a constant and welcome presence in his life. In a 2000 interview, Omidyar said, "I lived with my mom, but my dad was always around. I remember when I was younger spending weekends with my dad, who is a surgeon and medical doctor, doing rounds with him. We would spend maybe 45 minutes in the car going from one hospital to the next and we'd have some great conversations. That's one of my fond childhood memories."[5]

Because of the busy international schedule that his mother kept, Omidyar often traveled. He has even said that he never spent more than two or three years in one place until college.[6] By the time he reached the ninth grade, he was living in Hawaii. The frequent moves began to trouble him because of the difficulty in retaining old friends and constantly having to make new ones. "It was tough for me personally," he said.[7]

Typical of the plucky young man, however, he made the best of what was likely a tough situation. "There weren't a lot of kids around," he said. "And when I was younger I ended up hanging out with adults a lot more, because I had to."[8] That could help to explain how, at such a young age, Omidyar was able to excel in a business climate with people much older than he was. He did pay a price for being around adults only, however. "In retrospect I may have been cheated a little bit on the childhood side." But, he said, "I kind of grew up very quickly and became a little more mature more quickly than I see some of my relatives these days."[9]

EARLY INTEREST IN TECHNOLOGY AND COMPUTERS

While in the United States, Omidyar's interest in computers and technology grew. He was a self-described "typical nerd or geek."[10] It was certainly a good time to be interested in electronics. Just a decade before his birth, electronics in the home were mostly limited to televisions and stereos. In the 1970s, however, new devices came out on the market, such as pocket calculators and hand-held computer game devices. They were possible to manufacture because researchers learned how to better manage electricity and to use it to control what today seem like basic operations, such as operating the number pad on a calculator.

Young Omidyar was fascinated by these devices. "I was actually interested in gadgets, little electronic gadgets," he said. "I always managed to break them for one reason or another, of course, as kids do, and then I would take them apart and try to fix them, which I was never able to."[11]

OMIDYAR'S FIRST COMPUTER

Young students today grow up with computers, but computers were just beginning to show up in the market during Omidyar's childhood. The first computer he used was the TRS-80 model from RadioShack. It did not even belong to him. One of his teachers had the computer stashed away in a closet. Omidyar used to sneak out of gym class just to play around with the device.

Play turned into serious work because he soon learned how to program on it using the programming language BASIC.

Omidyar used his computer skills in a high school job. For six dollars an hour he created a computer program that would print out library cards for his school library's card catalog. The program formatted information that someone

⬆ The RadioShack TRS-80 personal computer that Omidyar first used sold for just under $600 in 1977. With just a fraction of the memory computers have today, it was certainly basic. Shortly thereafter, RadioShack sold an improved model, which bore a greater resemblance to the computers of today.

BASIC

BASIC is the acronym for Beginner's All-purpose Symbolic Instruction Code. Two Dartmouth College mathematicians created this computer programming language in 1963. They used it as a teaching tool to instruct their students about simple computing methods.

Personal computers would not become available until many years later, but the government, certain organizations, and businesses utilized gigantic early computers to manage important files, documents, and machinery. Paul Allen and Bill Gates, the founders of software giant Microsoft, utilized BASIC when creating their Altair computer, the first-ever device to be sold by Microsoft. Other, more complex computer programs have been created since the early 1960s, but some programmers still use BASIC and it remains a popular first computer language for students who are interested in technology.

typed into the system. (In those days, library users had to look up books and materials by shuffling through the organized cards that made up the card catalog.) It made organizing the catalog easier because all of the data on the cards appeared in a specific order.

Omidyar also programmed software to help with the scheduling of classes while he was in the tenth and eleventh grades. Similar to the card catalog formatting, he had to instruct the computer to create fields where people could type in information. The data could then be formatted, sorted, and organized. He jokingly admitted, "I resisted the temptation to [put some code in there] to make sure I never had classes on Friday, because I wouldn't have been able to get away with it, but I thought about it."[12]

Even though he was an apparent computer wizard at a very young age, and at a time when most students were not very interested in computers, Omidyar claims he did not receive straight As. He actually admitted that he was not a very good student because he did not study as much as he should have.[13] His test scores and grades, however, were sufficient for him to be admitted into Tufts University in Medford, Massachusetts, near Boston. The university would help to shape practically every aspect of his life, from his family values to eBay to his worldview.

CHAPTER TWO

UNIVERSITY LIFE AND EARLY CAREER

Interestingly, the international and cosmopolitan atmosphere of Tufts University somewhat mirrored that of Pierre Omidyar's Paris beginnings. According to the university, approximately 40 percent of all undergraduates at Tufts choose to study or work abroad. Omidyar, however, did not choose to do this, probably because he had already traveled so much. Tufts was also known for its strong language studies program, a field that Omidyar knew about from his mother and his own international upbringing. In addition, the university had a tight community within the larger urban setting of nearby Boston. The social scene at Tufts, therefore, must have captured, to some extent, the atmosphere of his life in Paris.

Omidyar claims he was not a very impressive student even in college. He seems to be genuinely proud that he graduated with a 3.0, or B, average, which is good but not extraordinary.

The Tufts University campus was where Omidyar apparently absorbed much of his business ethics. Modeled as an organization that respects diversity of opinion, community, and a fair work ethic, Tufts had a philosophy that translated into the business model that eBay would eventually practice.

"It was actually 3.01," he mockingly boasted. "During my entire four years there at Tufts my GPA improved every single semester, which gives you an idea of where I started. No, I was not a good student."[1]

TUFTS'S CORE VALUES

He may not always have paid proper attention to his studies, but quite a few influences from Tufts seem to have stuck with Omidyar. The university outlines a vision statement on its Web site. Later, in official speeches, eBay business meetings, and interviews, Omidyar repeatedly praised the values that the university practiced. He even incorporated them into the structure of eBay.

The first value in Tufts's vision statement is citizenship. "As an institution, we are committed to improving the human condition through education and discovery," the school Web site reads. "Beyond this commitment, we will strive to be a model for society at large."[2] If you have ever listened to Omidyar talk about his vision for eBay, that value should ring a bell.

Next, the university lists diversity. "We value a diverse community of women and men of different races, religions, geographic origins, socioeconomic backgrounds, sexual orientations, personal characteristics, and interests—where differences are understood and respected."[3] Omidyar preaches diversity and practices what he preaches. The employees he hired came from diverse cultural and ethnic backgrounds. Also, the users and listings at eBay reflect every imaginable interest and community.

Global orientation is the next value. The Tufts site says, "We will cultivate in our students an understanding of the citizens and cultures of the world . . . We will strive to contribute to global intellectual capital, harmony, and well-being."[4] Omidyar again has echoed this view in his public statements and through his work. He meant eBay to be more than just a place where people could buy and sell goods. Omidyar envisioned an idealistic community consisting of users from all around the world.

The final value listed by Tufts in its vision statement is fiscal responsibility. The university strives to pursue "policies that ensure fiscal soundness, now and in the future."[5] Money and success, as Omidyar would often suggest, can come and go quickly. If poorly managed, even a lot of money can disappear before you know it. Possessing billions of dollars, as Omidyar now does, would seem to quell such concerns, but he still strives for fiscal responsibility, and perhaps even more so now that he has a lot of money to manage.

A REVELATION

While the values at Tufts were slowly sinking in with Omidyar, a memorable experience occurred in his life. For many, a memorable experience is the discovery of a new singer or movie that they love, or finding a school subject, sport, or hobby that piques their intense curiosity. One of Pierre Omidyar's most memorable Tufts moments was when he taught himself how to program Apple's Macintosh computer.

Omidyar gravitated to Apple's products while at Tufts. In what he called a "weed out" computer science class (a class that determined whether students would be able progress to other levels in the subject), he first learned how to program in a computer language known simply as C.[6] Early computer programmers often used letters to name their programs. One early program was called BCPL, with the B probably coming from an early computer program nicknamed "bon." Improvements to those early programs resulted in C. The C programming language is still common today. "I learned how to program C," Omidyar said, "and then I used that ability to teach myself how to program the Macintosh, which I was just very excited about learning everything I could about it."[7]

Computers were not all that was on Omidyar's mind when he was at college. He was a member of Tuft's film club, and there he met a biology major from Hawaii named Pamela Wesley. She was part of the class of 1989. Omidyar was in the class of 1988. After graduating from Tufts, Wesley moved to California where she worked as a marketing consultant. In California she also reconnected with Omidyar, who later asked her for her hand in marriage. She accepted.

A BREAK FROM TUFTS

Numerous university students choose to study abroad during their junior year to gain new experiences in a different environment. Tufts had renowned overseas programs, and many of its students traveled abroad. Omidyar, however, instead of traveling abroad, stayed at Tufts, planning to work during the summers as a Macintosh

APPLE COMPUTERS

Apple today is famous for its computers as well as its related electronic gadgets, such as the iPod. However, like eBay, Apple had a humble start. In a garage in 1976, Steve Jobs and Steve Wozniak invented a microprocessor computer board, which is the main part of the computer that operates on data. They called the board the Apple I and sold it to friends, acquaintances, and locals who were interested in electronic devices. The next year, the two men founded Apple Computer, Inc. Later in 1977, they introduced the world's first personal computer, the Apple II.

We take for granted today that all computers should have a fair amount of memory, a keyboard, a mouse or some other navigational tool, and user-friendly graphics. Before the Apple II, these

Steve Jobs, a cofounder of Apple Computer, introduces the world's first personal computer, the Apple II, in 1979. A chess game is displayed on the screen. Other computers of the time had few, if any, graphics.

features were rare or nonexistent in computers, which were not designed for use by the general public, but rather for the government and corporations. The screens on these pre-Apple computers were only one color, the operating systems were often complex, and few people thought of them as sources of entertainment or tools for schoolwork. The Apple II, with its colorful display and visuals, was much more inviting.

Apple Computer, Inc., sold this first PC, or personal computer, for $1,290,[8] which can still buy you a basic Apple notebook computer today. The Apple II is obsolete now, but in 1977 it represented a monumental leap in technology. By the mid-1980s, when Omidyar was still attending Tufts, Apple had become one of America's fastest-growing companies. It had the initial edge over competing manufacturers like Wang Laboratories, which tended to market computers that stuck with more traditional, colorless graphics in hopes of appealing more to business users. Bill Gates adapted Apple technology for his machines and Microsoft software programs. Apple, as revealed through its innovative advertising, fancied itself more of a rebellious company with a youthful, modern personality. That image remains to this day.

Apple Computer became such a trendsetter in the mid-1980s that the famous pop artist Andy Warhol created this image called Apple. It praised the company's Macintosh computer.

computer programmer. After searching the classifieds in the Apple users' magazine *MacWorld*,
Omidyar came up with a list of companies that
interested him. He then sent out letters along
with a copy of his programmer's utility, which is
a program designed to perform or facilitate rou-
tine operations on a computer.

Omidyar was invited to serve as an intern
at Innovative Data Design in California's Silicon
Valley. At the time, computer experts were interested in devising programs that would allow
users to interact with their machines as though
they were using well-known writing implements,
such as pen, paper, drafting boards, and sketch
pads. Innovative Data Design's focus was on programs that enabled individuals to draw pictures
and graphics with Macintosh computers.

Omidyar was successful as an intern and
was offered a full-time job, which he accepted.
He did not go to Tufts for the 1988 fall semester
and instead remained in California. He was a
perfect fit for Silicon Valley. As a libertarian, he
even fit in with some of the area's more demo-
cratic political views.[9] Libertarians believe in free
will and an individual's right to have unrestricted
freedom in his or her thoughts and actions.

Omidyar even looked the part of the hip Silicon Valley computer expert, with his then long hair, beard, and stylish glasses.

Without a university degree, Omidyar had completed a successful internship and obtained a full-time job in the nation's hottest job market of the time. He still, however, wanted to earn his degree. He returned to Tufts for a semester. The lure of California again overtook him though, so he packed his bags and moved west, this time intending to stay on a permanent basis. He wound up finishing his undergraduate work at the University of California at Berkeley, located north of Silicon Valley.

At this stage, he could have continued his education. His mother, for example, earned several degrees beyond the basic four years of university study. Omidyar instead opted to throw himself into his computer work. The decision, for him, turned out to be a wise one, as another Apple subsidiary named Claris took an interest in the young computer whiz.

CHAPTER THREE

A REVOLUTIONARY IDEA

Pierre Omidyar's experience at Claris turned out to be a setback that could have led to a downward spiral; instead, he turned it into an opportunity.

Claris was a firm that developed consumer applications software. However, Omidyar was likely not as interested in the firm's products as he was in the prospect of the company going public, or being sold to investors on the stock market. Going public meant that virtually anyone could invest in the firm by buying its stock, or partial ownership in the company. If the company went public, Omidyar had the potential to make a lot of money.

Claris's future fizzled, however, since Apple wound up taking control of the company instead of having it go public. As a result, many of its employees, including Omidyar, were laid off. Omidyar, though, got together with some friends and a former Claris colleague in 1991 to found a company. They called it Ink Development Corporation.

INK DEVELOPMENT CORPORATION

The goal at Ink Development Corporation was to develop software that would enable people to operate computers using a pen stylus instead of a keyboard and mouse. At the time, this seemed like a great idea, but it never really caught on for desktop computers. Palm, Inc., the company that makes the Palm Pilot, a personal digital assistant (PDA), had some success with the technology, but this success never crossed over into more mainstream computing. These failures were a problem. Omidyar turned this problem into an opportunity—or, as the saying goes, he turned lemons into lemonade.

A side project at Ink Development Corporation involved creating software to manage

A businessman in this photograph uses a Palm Pilot during a meeting. This particular model has a stylus, or a penlike instrument, which allows users to enter functions on the machine. Omidyar envisioned such devices as early as the mid-1990s. He was way ahead of his time.

online shopping. As a result, Omidyar and his colleagues ditched the name Ink Development Corporation and renamed the firm eShop. The renamed company enjoyed a fair amount of success. A lot of people would have just settled into such a relatively stress-free job, but Omidyar wanted to take on other challenges. He left eShop in 1994 but retained a lot of control over the company. Then, in 1996, the software giant Microsoft bought eShop. Being one of the company's founders, Omidyar earned over a million dollars from the deal.

As a financially secure twenty-something, Omidyar now had more freedom to pursue other work that interested him. He became a software engineer for General Magic, an Apple offshoot. During his off hours from General Magic, Omidyar tinkered at home with his own software creation, AuctionWeb.

AUCTIONWEB

AuctionWeb was revolutionary. Though it followed an ancient, time-tested system of doing business—trading—AuctionWeb applied this system to the Internet. Omidyar envisioned the future attraction and the civic importance of such an operation. "If you think about it, commerce and trade is at the base of all human activity . . . in the old days people would bring their stuff to market and they'd do business and then they'd go back to their hillside home or wherever."[1] He then went on to explain that, as time went on, the vendors became so inundated with customers that walls were built around them. This, he said, contributed to the birth of cities and large societies.

AuctionWeb Categories

New Today	Ending Today	Completed	Search!
Collecting	**Computer Hardware**	**Computer Software**	**Other**
Antiques (over 100 years) (504)	General (515)	General (593)	Audio Equipment (84)
Antiques (less than 100 years) (2909)	Books (16)	Books (85)	Automotive (83)
Art (214)	CPUs (238)	Business (70)	Clothing (184)
Autographs (504)	Drives (281)	Educational (144)	Consumer Electronics (199)
Books, Magazines (1771)	Input Periphs. (80)	Games (496)	Erotic, Adults Only (258)
Clocks and Timepieces (266)	Macintosh (129)	Graphics & Multimedia (92)	Jewelry, Gemstones (498)
Coins, Currency, Certificates - Non U.S. (276)	Memory (97)	Macintosh (157)	Movies, LaserDiscs, etc. (324
Coins, Currency, Certificates - U.S. (968)	Modems (73)	Sega, Nintendo, etc. (388)	Photography, Video Equipme (299)
Comics (706)	Multimedia (107)	Utilities (49)	Records, Tapes, CDs (655)
Costume Jewelry (585)	Networking (53)		Services (19)
Decorative, Kitchenware, Pottery (2365)	Printers (96)		Sporting Goods (175)
Figures, Dolls (1493)	Video (125)		Travel (7)
Figures, Dolls: Action Figures (856)			Miscellaneous (326)
Figures, Dolls: Barbie & Accessories (832)			

Most of the general product categories were present not long after AuctionWeb first appeared on the Internet. Computer hardware and software offerings initially dominated the online auction. The reason for this was that technology buffs, like Omidyar himself, were the first to own computers and, therefore, were the first to frequent AuctionWeb.

Omidyar's interest, however, was more in the human rather than the historical side of commerce. Because the interactions between buyer and seller were purely online, they probably mirrored the online discussions he himself had enjoyed as a frequent participant in Usenet.

THE LASER PEN THAT DIDN'T WORK

One of the first items to go up for sale on AuctionWeb was a laser pointer that Omidyar himself owned. He planned to use it for presentations, flashing it at documents or visuals, but he never did end up using it much except as a cat toy for his resident feline. The device broke, but he listed it on AuctionWeb anyway. "Broken Laser Pointer," the heading read. The description field explained that Omidyar paid $30 for the useless device. After a couple of weeks, an individual bid on the pointer. By the end of the auction, the bidding had reached $14, which was not bad for a gizmo that was no longer even operable. The successful sale of this apparently unwanted device was an indication of the future success of Omidyar's auction business.

COMPUTERS AND COLLECTIBLES

Most of the early AuctionWeb items for sale had to do with computers and electronics. That seemed natural, given that these were Omidyar's own interests and the pastimes of his friends. However, it did not take long before other types of nonelectronic items and collectibles appeared in auctions on the Web site. AuctionWeb visitors had the choice of bidding on an incredibly diverse, and one might say slightly odd, group of items. These first offerings included a cast-iron hook and ladder truck, a Superman metal lunch-box from 1967, a 1989 Toyota Tercel with 64,000 miles (102,998 kilometers), a comic book, some computer game equipment, and even a "Presidential Premier GOLD" membership to a Chicago health club.[2]

In 2000, eBay auctioned off these boxing shoes, which belonged to boxing legend Muhammad Ali. The fighter wore them during his first bout with Joe Frazier on March 8, 1971. Bids began at over $100,000, which showed how much money was being transacted on the growing auction site.

Omidyar allowed people to use the services of AuctionWeb for free. Sellers just posted their items for sale and buyers paid the winning bid price. Money, therefore, was only exchanged between the buyer and the seller. For buyers and sellers then, it was a win-win situation. Sellers, like Omidyar, could get cash for items they didn't want that they wished to exchange for money. In addition, bidders competed with each other, as though they were in a sporting match. If they won, they likely felt the thrill of victory.

As word spread about AuctionWeb, increasing numbers of people gravitated to the site. The heavy online traffic overwhelmed Omidyar's Internet service provider (ISP), Best. The ISP contacted Omidyar and complained about the overload. As a result, Best hiked up his monthly fee to $250. Omidyar, who viewed the project as a fun, free hobby, now had to start thinking of it as a business. He had to figure out a way to keep the service running with this new expense. He would continually lose money if he were the only one to foot the bill for the site.

To recoup his ISP costs, Omidyar decided to charge fees to his sellers. The first fees were 5 percent of the sale price for items that sold for less than $25. For items that sold for $25 and above, the fee was 2.5 percent of the sale price.[3] Unlike a standard business, Omidyar did not have a collection service at his disposal to make sure that fees would be paid. When fees were first issued, the procedure was based on an honor system, where sellers were simply expected to pay the money they owed.

Who knew that such a simple system would eventually lead to extraordinary riches? Omidyar never predicted the financial windfall. That first month he collected well over the $250 Best was charging him. With little advertising and personal financial investment, he was already turning a profit, and the money kept pouring in, along with new AuctionWeb users.

By March of 1995, Omidyar was earning $1,000 of profit per month. In April, that figure more than doubled to $2,500. In May, he saw profits rise to $5,000, and in June he made $10,000.[4] AuctionWeb's growth was extraordinary. What's even more astonishing is that this growth came at a time when many start-up Internet businesses with high hopes wound up failing. Omidyar hardly had to leave his home or do any extra work with each subsequent month. Without a doubt, his online auction site was a resounding success.

Internet Service Providers

An Internet service provider, or ISP, is a company that connects an individual's computer to the Internet. The Internet, in turn, is a global network of computers. Users need a modem, or some other device such as a digital subscriber line (DSL), cable, Ethernet, or wireless connection, to enable them to connect to the Internet through the ISP. Sometimes ISPs will provide these devices. In other instances, computer users rely upon their own connections, communicating with the ISP through a phone line or a television cable hookup.

THE FEEDBACK FORUM

Initially, users of AuctionWeb e-mailed Omidyar whenever they had complaints, wanted to ask questions, or otherwise wanted to comment about the site. Since Omidyar posted his e-mail address prominently on the site, most of the messages were directed to him. However, he preferred to deal with buyer-seller disputes by having the complaining parties work out the matter amongst themselves. He, after all, was only the overseer of the site. He did not directly participate in the transactions.

The way Omidyar dealt with this problem was by adding what he called the Feedback

Forum to the site. The Feedback Forum was a place online where users could publicly post comments about buyers and sellers. A seller who experienced a good transaction, for example, might jot down a complimentary note about the buyer, while a buyer dissatisfied with his or her purchase could voice a negative opinion about the seller. Buyers and sellers had the right to question comments, but usually the comments remained part of the individual's permanent transaction record.

Omidyar proposed his Feedback Forum idea less than a year after the site's launch in February 1996. His announcement, posted at the Web site, read, "Most people are honest. However, some people are dishonest. Or deceptive. This is true here, in the newsgroups, in the classifieds, and right next door. It's a fact of life. But here, those people can't hide. We'll drive them away. Protect others from them. This grand hope depends on your active participation. Become a registered user. Use our Feedback Forum. Give praise where it is due; make complaints where appropriate . . . Deal with others the way you would have them deal with you. Remember that you are usually dealing with individuals, just like yourself. Subject to making

Auction Web

[Menu] [Listings] [Add your item] [Search]

The AuctionWeb Bulletin Board

This page contains messages left by AuctionWeb registered users. You can use this bulletin board to communicate with the rest of the AuctionWeb community. Only the most recent **100** messages will be kept. (This used to be higher, but this page became too slow.)

Don't forget about our other features:

- If you want to leave a complaint or praise about another user, please use the **user feedback forum**.
- If you want to make a request for someone to sell a particular item, please use the **Wanted page**.

Jump to the message list

Add a new message

You must be a registered user to leave a message. For your protection, you also need a password in order to leave a message. If you are already registered but you haven't selected a personal password, or if you've forgotten your password, please request a new temporary password before proceeding.

You are responsible for your own words. Messages cannot be removed once they have been posted. Please consider your message carefully before submitting it.

Your registered e-mail address: [   ]
Your password: [   ]

Your message (no HTML):

Press this button to save your listing:

    save message

Press this button to clear the form if you made a mistake:

    clear form

The AuctionWeb Bulletin Board

User: bd_wood (9) **Date:** 10/02/96 **Time:** 17:32:19 PDT	My two cents worth to the saga of too much drivel. If you want pat answers to your questions, try the FAQ's area. If you like a little lighthearted banter the BB is the place to be. If the cost is too extreme get an online service that offers unlimited access. Bruce :-Þ P.S. :-Þ (see all the neat things you can

The AuctionWeb bulletin board was a precursor to eBay's groundbreaking Feedback Forum. Here, users could vent their anger about bad transactions or praise the site about good ones, as the form encouraged. The board promoted community involvement and, in terms of business, allowed buyers and sellers to police one another.

mistakes. Well-meaning, but wrong on occasion. That's just human."[5]

THE IMPORTANCE OF AUCTIONWEB

Omidyar accomplished many goals with AuctionWeb. First, by establishing one of the first Feedback Forums, Omidyar ensured that the auction service could better operate on its own, with little or no seller-buyer management required from himself or other workers, especially in the potentially difficult matter of resolving disputes. He took the burden of proof away from himself and the site and placed it back in the hands of the very people who were using the service. Because of this, the Feedback Forum emerged as a new self-policing system that revolutionized e-commerce.

Secondly, Omidyar used AuctionWeb to encourage buyers and sellers to become registered users. To this day, this is a controversial issue in online commerce. Brick-and-mortar stores do not require registration. You can simply walk through the doors, pay cash for an item, and walk out without leaving any personal information. Online registration, though, often requires a lot of personal information that the buyer might not want to offer for security reasons, including

Traditional retail stores, such as this Wal-Mart in San Antonio, Texas, provide customers with a number of payment options. The Internet, however, often requires that buyers and sellers use only credit cards or an online payment service, such as PayPal. These payment types are usually secure, but they do allow other businesses, even the companies that issued the credit cards, to document purchases. Some people feel that this invades their right to privacy.

credit card numbers, Social Security numbers, phone numbers, and home addresses. Many consumers fear that companies may use the information to track a person's buying patterns or even sell that personal information to outside firms. Often, online registration is viewed as a benefit more to the company than to the consumer. In the case of AuctionWeb, registration seemed to benefit users and the company mutually. Omdiyar was able to gather data to better maintain the site while users could check the feedback of buyers and sellers to determine if people were, as Omidyar warned, dishonest or deceptive.

Finally, AuctionWeb broke ground in that it was not just another retail site. As Omidyar had hoped and envisioned, it was developing into its own ever-expanding community without walls, harsh restrictions, and social hierarchies. The wording of Omidyar's Feedback Forum announcement almost sounded like that of a caring relative or friend. One of the amazing things about communicating via the Internet is that strangers from all around the world can meet at one place to conduct business or even to express themselves. Unexpected friendships often develop, which lead to widespread virtual communities. At the time, at least, the auction site came to represent Omidyar's idealized version of what communities could, and should, become.

Chapter Four

AuctionWeb Renames Itself

A uctionWeb users always accessed the service through the URL http://www.ebay.com. Initially the AuctionWeb site was one of three that Omidyar operated as home pages on http://www.ebay.com. It is fairly easy to create such pages to display photographs or to share information about your favorite subjects. Aside from AuctionWeb, Omidyar created a page for his fiancée, Pam Wesley, which had data pertaining to a small biotechnology start-up firm that she was working for as a management consultant.

The http://www.ebay.com site also linked to a page on the Ebola virus. Called Ebola Information, the page had all sorts of links and information pertaining to the deadly disease. It is unclear why Omidyar created the page. Regardless, there is an apparent similarity between the words "Ebola" and "eBay." Since people then would have been more familiar with the word "Ebola," perhaps he wished to capture some of the traffic searching for information on the virus, hoping that they would then gravitate to the http://www.ebay.com URL. It also might have just been a bit of dark humor to contrast eBay with the other two sites he ran.

Traffic to AuctionWeb far surpassed that to the other sites. Omidyar dumped the other two sites since it was probably awkward for users who were looking for an online auction to see information on Ebola and a biotech company. In September 1997, Omidyar dropped the name "AuctionWeb" and used just "eBay."

THE ONLINE FAMILY GROWS

Since eBay relied so much on its users, it is no wonder that strong relationships were forged between users of the site, particularly in the few years after it was launched. Omidyar himself had

Home | Listings | Buyers | Sellers | Search | Help | Cafe | Site Map

Featured

"Beatles* 1964 Hards Days Night Button at $8.99

Safety Can Opener — One Of Its Kind!! at $7.99

Cute Glass Reindeer Ornament (Photo) at $9.99

more featured...

eBay

Welcome to the leading person-to-person auction community on the web!

list an item for sale   chat in the cafe

Register. Join the party.
Tutorial. Learn to use eBay. NEW!

eBay Stats

138,054 items for sale in 371 categories!

3,623,170 items for sale on eBay since inception!

14,726,796 bids made since inception!

Over 3,000,000 page views per day!

User Spotlight

Comments about
jaguar@kans.com (54) ☆

"A++ will definatly do business again"

"very good to deal with. quick and easy fast reply's and payment thank-you"

"Fast E-Mail...Fast Pay...Aaa+"

eBay Categories

Antiques (pre-1900) *(2111)*

Computers *(7947)*

Trading Cards *(11047)*

Dolls, Figures *(8488)*

Stamps *(2319)*

Jewelry, Gemstones *(6078)*

all listings...

Collectibles *(58861)*

Memorabilia *(6233)*

Toys *(14487)*

Coins *(2754)*

Books, Magazines *(6315)*

Miscellaneous *(11412)*

Last updated: 11/17/97, 11:01:17 PST

DISNEY CONTEST!

Member of the Internet Link Exchange

Netscape NOW!

FREE Microsoft Internet Explorer

The home page for eBay in early 1997 looked rather plain and humble when compared to today's flashier version. Even back then, however, the site's popularity was impressive. Millions of items were already up for auction and were sold on eBay. Today, that number has grown well into the billions.

ORIGIN OF THE NAME "EBAY"

Omidyar enjoys outdoor sporting activities, such as snowboarding at Lake Tahoe and other popular sites in the west. At some point, he learned about Echo Bay, Nevada. Located near the state's Lake Mead, Echo Bay is a wilderness area frequented by campers, hikers, and vacationers. In addition to his fondness for the place itself , Omidyar says the name Echo Bay "just sounded cool."[1] As a result, he initially tried to use the name for his Web site. He tried to include the full name in his Web address as echobay.com, but a mining company in Canada had already registered the URL. He then tried to register http://www.ebay.com. This time the registration went through. The URL http://www.ebay.com and the name eBay have stuck ever since.

enjoyed using his computer as a communications tool long before most people saw the potential. As a Usenet member, he shared Apple computer programming information with other members he became acquainted with through the computer. People just enjoyed communicating with others online. Sometimes these relationships even led to face-to-face meetings.

What was so unusual about eBay's community was that it was founded as a site dedicated to shopping, which is often a relatively impersonal, business-oriented activity. In its early years, eBay turned around this notion that shopping must be an impersonal practice. In some ways, the site was even more effective at encouraging new friendships than, say, shopping in malls or brick-and-mortar stores.

Some of the early people at eBay were busy, social individuals who casually posted chatty messages associated with their auction activity. Other people had more time on their hands. At eBay they not only found a place to shop, but also a warm and inviting virtual environment within which they could find friends and companionship. "Uncle Griff" was one such character.

UNCLE GRIFF

In 1996, the bulletin board of the then-fledgling AuctionWeb mainly included messages asking questions about the site's service. Omidyar answered quite a few of these questions on his own, but since the board was open to anyone, other people started to chip in and provide answers themselves. One regular responder called himself "Uncle Griff." Based upon his responses, Uncle Griff knew a lot about computers. Instead of just writing dry, technical answers to computer or AuctionWeb questions, however, he peppered his responses with humor. He even created a silly, outrageous online character for himself. As an example of just how outrageous this character was, one AuctionWeb user once asked him what he looked like. Uncle Griff replied, masquerading as a female, that he was wearing a "lovely flower print dress and I just got through milking the cows."[2]

In reality, Uncle Griff was Jim Griffith, a decorator and painter with a fondness for computing who had fallen on tough financial times. He provided help on AuctionWeb for free, which allowed him to socialize and have a little fun. After a while, depression set in for Griffith and he stopped posting to the bulletin board. His presence was certainly missed by users and the company itself. As a result, the company contacted Griffith and offered him a job as a speaker at seminars of the newly formed eBay University. These were conferences offered to newcomers on how to buy and sell on the site. He accepted and is still associated with eBay today.

Other community members, such as a woman nicknamed "Aunt Patti," regularly joined in on the bulletin board exchanges. Users either joined the community by regularly posting messages themselves, or, at the very least, they counted on individuals like Uncle Griff and Aunt Patti to give them a laugh and help them with their auction problems. Like the Feedback

eBay

home | pay | register | site map

| Buy | Sell | My eBay | Community | Help |

Start new search [Search]
Advanced Search

Java™ POWERED BY ◆Sun
TECHNOLOGY

Home > Help > eBay University > **Meet the Instructors**

eBay University

Choose A Topic

Welcome
Online Courses
Attend Classes
Meet the Instructors
Griff's Corner
Education Specialist Program

Related Links

Help
Learning Center

Meet the Instructors

Get to know the eBay University instructors! Although they come to you from a variety of backgrounds, the one thing they have in common is that they actively buy and sell on eBay, and are passionate about teaching others how to 'Do it eBay'!

Griff - Dean of eBay Education	Michael Kaiser	Patti "Louise" Ruby
Marsha Collier	Brian Lierz	Catherine Seda
Janelle Elms	Steve Lindhorst	Christopher Spencer
Cliff Ennico	Jason Miner	Jack Waddick
Ted Janusz	Scott Pribyl	

Jim Griffith

"Griff," as he is popularly known, has been the foremost education expert on eBay since 1996 when he was invited to join the company as its first customer support representative. For the past three years in his role as both eBay ambassador and instructor, Griff has been traveling around the country leading eBay University seminars and attending community gatherings on how to buy and sell on eBay.

With his intimate knowledge of every aspect of eBay, Griff educates people on everything from basic search tips to growing a serious business on eBay. Most importantly, he makes learning eBay fun and easy.

Using plain English and a sense of humor to put his audiences at ease, Griff can teach anyone-timid computer novice or long-time eBay seller alike-how to make their eBay searching, shopping and selling more effective.

Griff has shared his eBay expertise with audiences across the country. In addition to presenting at dozens of eBay University events, he's made more than 100 local and national television and radio appearances.

Griff is also the author of the *Official eBay Bible* and host of *eBay Radio*.

⬆ Jim Griffith, otherwise known as Uncle Griff, served as the Dean of eBay Education and was one of the company's key players. Many other instructors, however, have since worked at eBay and continue to do so at the site's current online university. There, interested individuals can learn all about buying, selling, and strategies for improving their profits.

Forum, Omidyar's brilliant bulletin board system was a means to resolve potentially serious problems. In the case of the bulletin board, Omidyar was saved the hassle of having to answer each and every question personally. The community took care of itself.

THE EBAY STAFF

Omidyar's official staff at eBay, although small in number, came to reflect the diverse, close-knit nature of the Web site's community of users. When Omidyar quit his job at General Magic, he looked for business partners. One he eventually settled on was a man named Jeff Skoll, who was a Canadian-born graduate of Stanford University's prestigious business school. Skoll, like Omidyar, was not just interested in making money. He was truly fascinated by computers, technology, and the emerging opportunities offered by the Internet. Skoll worked long hours. Even when he became a multibillionaire through eBay, like Omidyar, Skoll chose to live in a small rental house with four roommates and hardly bought anything for himself with his incredible new fortune.

Another important team member was Mary Lou Song, a young Korean-American woman with a degree in journalism. Skoll and Omidyar hired Song as eBay's public relations manager to handle the company's relationship with the press and other media. She was not as well versed in computers and technology as Omidyar and Skoll, but she brought a sharp eye and a common-sense approach to her job. Song, for example, was

A vintage photo of Elvis Presley hangs next to this senior customer accounts representative at work at eBay's San Jose, California, headquarters. Her casual attire suggests the relaxed, yet efficient, attitude that Omidyar promoted at his company. Perhaps most telling is the writing on her T-shirt. Even employees enjoy buying and selling on eBay.

largely responsible for transforming the Web site from a dull, colorless series of text-filled pages to the bright, vibrant, and highly visual eBay of today, which includes large, full-color photographs of items on auction where only text descriptions used to exist.

With Griffith, Skoll, Song, and a handful of others, Omidyar had created a small yet winning team devoted to its colleagues and its customers. However, in order for eBay to grow and prosper, the company needed financial backing from outside investors. While at Ink Development Corporation, Omidyar had worked with Bruce Dunlevie, who later became one of the founders of Benchmark Capital, a venture capital firm based in Silicon Valley. Venture capitalists are individuals or groups who directly invest in companies as opposed to simply buying stock in them. The investment is often very risky for the venture capitalists, but if the company receiving the funding later generates large profits, the venture capitalists can earn a large amount of money.

Omidyar did not have much of a business plan to begin with, which is understandable given that eBay originated in a living room one weekend. He and his colleagues even had to jot down a makeshift plan in order to rent their first office. Their real focus was on the programming involved and the people who used the Web site, instead of a company strategy. Investors, however, like to see business plans. They often

From left to right are Bruce Dunlevie, Kevin Harvey, Andrew Rachleff, Robert Kagle, and David Beirne. All of these men were general partners at Benchmark Capital, which first invested in eBay. Aside from its unbelievable success due to a 30 percent stake in Omidyar's auction business, the firm also helped to launch AOL, among other technology giants at the time.

contribute millions of dollars to start-ups and want to make sure that these unproven companies will be successful. Dunlevie requested one from Omidyar, but Omidyar instead suggested that they meet for "old times' sake."[3]

BOB KAGLE

At their meeting, Dunlevie introduced Omidyar to Bob Kagle, one of his partners at Benchmark. Kagle grew up in Flint, Michigan, which is the home of General Motors. Kagle went to a school operated by the automobile manufacturer and was a hard-working businessman who was first drawn to California by a desire to study at Stanford. Omidyar's first meeting with Kagle, however, was somewhat of a disaster. Omidyar planned to let eBay sell itself by showing the site to the two men during the meeting. He failed, however, to bring his own computer and had to borrow one at Benchmark. When he typed in http://www.ebay.com, the site did not appear on the screen. The server had gone down, which was one reason why the auction site needed the funding in the first place. A high-power server and constant maintenance are required to run a busy site with many visitors. Although Omidyar spoke with conviction about his vision of creating an online community, Kagle left the meeting unimpressed.

What changed Kagle's mind was a later visit to the eBay site. As it turns out, Kagle collected hand-carved fish decoys, which are not exactly items that you would find in an average store at a shopping mall in most cities. In other words, they were hard to find. When Kagle signed on to eBay, which was working perfectly this time, he found many decoys for sale, including some he had never even seen before. He bid on one. Though he ultimately lost the bid, the eBay experience showed him how unique the company was. As a result, Benchmark Capital initially gave eBay $6.5 million in exchange for a portion of future profits. Although Kagle could see the site's potential, he probably never imagined that Benchmark's $6.5 million investment would eventually be worth over $1 billion.

CHAPTER FIVE

THE RIGHT PLACE AT THE RIGHT TIME

Less than fifty years ago, Silicon Valley's largest city, San Jose, existed in the shadow of San Francisco to the north. A famous song in 1967 was even titled, "Do You Know the Way to San Jose?" because many people from outside the area had either never heard of the city or did not know where it was located. A city that is spacious, yet without a glitzy reputation, has its perks, however. One of those perks is that real estate tends to be less expensive than

This sign in front of eBay's San Jose headquarters is posted with various categories of items that are up for auction on the Web site. Fun amusements such as these reflect eBay's casual attitude. They also symbolize the feeling that the online auction site has grown so popular that it can now be seen in every direction you turn.

in other, more popular areas. San Jose and its surrounding cities were relatively affordable by California standards in the early 1970s.

San Jose's proximity to Stanford University brought many young people with degrees in hand and an entrepreneurial spirit to the area. Xerox's research center in Palo Alto, which is just west of San Jose, also became an early draw for this type of person in the the 1970s, as did Apple Computer. These companies were themselves inspired by prior technological breakthroughs that many believe began as early as 1820 when British mathematician and inventor Charles Babbage created a mechanical computing machine called the Difference Engine. This simple, calculator-type device was formulated on principles that computers still use today.

More than 100 years and many other computer-related inventions later came another critical component. In 1977, inventor Dennis C. Hayes created the personal computer modem. It is almost impossible to fathom what computing would be like today without modems, which have allowed computers to connect to the Internet. Modems, in fact, were a key component in the growth of the Web.

What added to the growth of Silicon Valley businesses in the 1980s and 1990s was the new breed of electronic-related, or e-related, innovations such as e-mail and e-commerce. E-mail changed the way many of us communicate. E-mail allows buyers and sellers on eBay (which cleverly incorporates the "e" into its name) to communicate off the Web site, so personal information, such as addresses and phone numbers, can be exchanged outside of public view.

E-commerce was another innovation that began less than a few decades ago. E-commerce refers to the exchange of money, or something else of value, for goods and services over the Internet. Within e-commerce there are what are called business-to-business (B2B) transactions, which occur between two businesses rather than a consumer and a business. Consumer-to-business transactions include traditional online retailing, where a business sells a service or product to an individual.

Neither of these categories fits eBay, so "online auction" has now become recognized as its own type of e-commerce, one that involves buyers and sellers who utilize bidding strategies to determine the selling prices of goods.

eBay Leads to Other Business Growth

The popularity of eBay, as well as all forms of e-commerce, increased the business of shipping firms such as FedEx[1] and the United States Postal Service. These companies experienced tremendous profit increases in 1997 and 1998 thanks to all of the people and businesses shipping items from one place to another. Credit card companies, like American Express, also saw their profits jump, since so many individuals were charging items instead of paying for them with cash.

To facilitate payment for goods, e-commerce services like PayPal emerged and continue to flourish. If you take a look at many items offered for sale on eBay, you will notice that quite a few sellers list PayPal as a preferred method of payment. PayPal became so popular for payment on eBay that eBay eventually bought the company in 2002. The reason why PayPal is so popular is that it provides some security to buyers and sellers. Its members have to provide their credit card information and can become "verified" by PayPal, meaning that they have also provided information about their bank account. PayPal acts like a middleman between the buyer and the seller, which can eliminate

Since PayPal was the most preferred method for money transactions for its online auctions, eBay simply decided to buy the company in 2002. By making PayPal a part of the eBay team, eBay users now have an easier experience selling their items. A smoother user experience is at the heart of all of eBay's acquisitions.

some of the risk of paying or receiving directly from an unknown person or company.

Even businesses designed specifically to help people sell on eBay, such as iSOLD It, have sprung into action. Likely, someone in your area is operating one such business. While not required for doing business on eBay, these service companies can help you list, manage, and ship goods, particularly if you plan to sell many items in large quantities.

The ease of selling goods on eBay has even resulted in people creating their own eBay businesses. For example, a person might sell a few old comic books on the site. If he earns a good profit he might then decide to sell more. If income is sufficient, the seller might officially register the business's Web page on eBay's site. A business called House O'Laffs, for instance, might have a Web page that is linked to eBay. A person in another country may have never heard of House O'Laffs, but that person could go to the more familiar eBay, look for comic books, and then find House O'Laffs through an eBay search for comic books. Just as Omidyar left his day job because of the success he found through eBay, some sellers now work full-time selling on the eBay site.

THE COLLECTIBLES BOOM

People have always been interested in collectibles, but when collectibles started being sold on the Web, even individuals who otherwise had never frequented collectibles shops became consumers. Just as Bob Kagle found his rare fish decoys sold on eBay, people interested in antiques and collectibles from all around the world could link with each other to buy and sell these one-of-a-kind items. Before eBay, a person looking for a set of 1949 New York Yankees baseball cards, for example, probably wouldn't have been able to find it very easily. Now the person can search eBay from the comfort of his

Sue Dale *(right)* is clearly happy. Tara Finley *(left)*, an appraiser for the television show *Antiques Roadshow,* has just valued her 1920s penny arcade machine at $700. *Antiques Roadshow,* which helps people value their belongings, has helped to fuel interest in collectibles in recent years. It has also likely increased auctions for collectibles on eBay.

or her home and, over time, likely find someone somewhere offering to sell the desired cards.

Television programs like *Antiques Roadshow*, which shows appraisers determining the value of people's antiques, also generate interest in collectibles. *Antiques Roadshow* demonstrates the fact that one person's trash is often another person's treasure. An old stamp might be valueless to a person with an untrained eye, but to an expert, it could be worth thousands of dollars.

Suddenly everyone was digging through their attics and storage closets for such treasures. Many of these people went on eBay either hoping to find an item that would increase in value over time or hoping to sell products at top dollar during the collectibles boom. One such collectible that was popular when AuctionWeb launched was a certain type of stuffed toy. During one month alone in 1997, eBay sold $500,000 worth of them.[2] These collectibles were the now classic Beanie Babies.

To give some idea of how eBay capitalized on these trends, visits to the site rose from 600,000 to more than 2 million in a two-week period in 1996.[3] Many of these visitors liked what they saw and became registered eBay users. In 1997, the number of registered users doubled

Beanie Babies, the once-popular stuffed toys, are cradled in the arms of the creator of the stuffed animals H. Ty Warner. Although the toys were not expensive to make, they sometimes sold for thousands of dollars to collectors since they were often released in limited editions. Needless to say, eBay made a fortune from the Beanie Baby craze.

in just a six-month period.[4] These people then brought their friends, coworkers, and families to the site, so activity at eBay continued to rise.

THE FALL VISION TOUR

With nothing more than two simple announcements before its initial launch and little else in the way of promotion, eBay had become a

POWERSELLERS

Fees can add up for people who sell more than a few items at eBay, but they are of particular concern to PowerSellers, or sellers who sell in high volume on eBay. The site recognizes several levels of sales volumes, ranging from $1,000 a month in regular sales to over $150,000 a month. Individuals or vendors who fall within those ranges are invited by eBay to join the free PowerSellers club. One of the most obvious benefits to Power-Sellers is that a PowerSeller logo appears with their item listings. PowerSellers are also offered prioritized customer service, networking options, and special offers.

monumental success. In 1997, the company decided to test the public relations waters by conducting the most substantial promotional campaign in its history. Called the Fall Vision Tour, the promotion aimed to introduce Omidyar and eBay to reporters and industry experts. Omidyar, who seemed to prefer working behind the scenes, went ahead with the tour, which involved speeches, meetings, presentations, and reciting statistics pertaining to the company's success. The catchphrase of the tour, meant to draw the attention of the media, was "eBay is proven, fun, and safe."[5]

However, a few problems revealed themselves on the tour. Despite eBay's success, some television stations, newspapers, and magazines did not meet with Omidyar, feeling at the time that eBay was not yet newsworthy.[6] Another problem that cropped up on the tour was that Omidyar was asked about purported cases of fraud at eBay. He responded that instances of reported fraud were less frequent at the auction site than in standard retail stores.

This was an omen of future problems. Some years later, in 2001, eBay won a landmark lawsuit filed by Lars Gentry, who had unknowingly purchased fake sports memorabilia, such as items with forged autographs.[7] Gentry claimed that eBay was a "dealer" and should be held responsible for the authenticity of items sold on the site. Representatives of eBay argued back that it was just a venue for selling and not a dealer and therefore not responsible for the authenticity of items sold on the site. The judge dismissed the case, which could have cost eBay $100 million had eBay lost, and might have led to additional lawsuits.

The eBay Fall Vision Tour was not a complete failure, however, since it did result in some media and industry attention, but it was not a huge success either. Perhaps one reason was that the Web site had outgrown the relatively small, close communities that had forged in the AuctionWeb days. Omidyar performed best when the auction site retained this close-knit community; he did not appear to feel comfortable in the media spotlight that came with the company's success. However, big changes were ahead for both eBay and its founder.

Chapter Six

The Founder Steps Aside

A ll businesses, even large ones, must stay competitive and grow to survive and to continue to succeed. With investors now looking at eBay's profits, and Omidyar and Skoll wanting to push eBay to further success, the eBay team collectively decided to bring more money into the company by selling stock to the public. Stock, in the form of certificates, represents partial ownership of a corporation. When a corporation's stock is offered for sale to the public for the first time, the event is called an IPO, or an initial public offering.

Selling shares to the public meant that Omidyar and Skoll had to be more professional about the company's leadership. As Omidyar admitted, "We were entrepreneurs and that was good up to a certain stage, but we didn't have the experience to take the company to the next level."[1] They brought in a headhunter, someone who helped them look for top-quality leaders. They wanted people who had a proven record of accomplishment and the right level of interest and potential. Immediately, all eyes were on Meg Whitman.

MEG WHITMAN

Meg Whitman came from an elite Long Island, New York, family. Her father was involved in finance while her mother had gained some fame as a member of a women's delegation led by actress Shirley MacLaine. The delegation traveled to China in 1973, just after the country had opened itself a bit more to Western nations during President Richard Nixon's administration. With her father's business skills and her mother's confidence, Whitman followed an Ivy League route by first attending Princeton University and then earning an MBA, an advanced business degree, from Harvard University.

Pez candy dispensers are lined up like soldiers in front of Meg Whitman, eBay's chief executive officer. Whitman had been at the company for a little over a year when this photograph was taken in May 1999. She had already witnessed $2.4 million in profits and overseen a site that then had 3.8 million registered members.

Whitman had served as president of
Stride Rite shoes, FTD Flowers, and Playskool,
a toy manufacturer that is part of the larger
Hasbro Corporation. Playskool perhaps is most
famous as the manufacturer of the popular
Mr. Potato Head toys. Whitman was working
at Playskool when eBay's headhunters
approached her.

Like Kagle, Whitman was not interested in
eBay at first. As a busy executive, she had never
bought or sold anything on the site. Moreover,
her husband held an important position as a
brain surgeon at Massachusetts General
Hospital, near her office at Playskool. Still, she
agreed to be interviewed by Omidyar and his
colleagues; Uncle Griff later recalled that eBay
had to quickly hire a receptionist to work at
their sparse main office in the hopes of impress-
ing Whitman.[2] After her meeting, Whitman
was impressed with Omidyar, eBay's financial
records, and the financial offer she received,
one that she would eventually accept. In 1998,
Whitman became the CEO, or chief executive
officer, of eBay. Omidyar stayed on as founder
and chairman of the eBay board, a less involved,
but no less important, position.

THE IPO

Before an IPO, a company usually goes on a road show, or a tour, to promote the business. Similar to eBay's Fall Vision Tour, the goal of its road show was to drum up interest and publicity. In this case, it was also meant to target both professional and casual investors from the public. The investment firm Goldman Sachs, after some heated competition from other firms, won the right to handle the eBay IPO. Omidyar dreaded the publicity tour, but he had Goldman Sachs foot the bill and made the most of it. With Whitman now holding the title of CEO of eBay, Omidyar was at least able to let her do most of the talking and media work.

In 1998, when the IPO finally took place, Omidyar, Whitman, Skoll, and others waited anxiously at the Goldman Sachs offices in New York. By the end of the day, every executive in that room at Goldman Sachs became very rich. The IPO sold more than $2 billion worth of eBay stock.[3]

THE COMPANY'S CONTINUED GROWTH

Today, the eBay empire continues to grow. In 2005, the company invested in Skype, an Internet

When eBay went public in 1998, it was listed on the NASDAQ, a stock exchange that trades the shares of technology companies such as Yahoo!, Dell, and Microsoft. EBay was a natural fit for the NASDAQ since many of the companies it was listed along-side were young and cutting-edge.

telephone firm, for $2.6 billion. If Skype's profits rise in the next three years, eBay will pay the company an additional $1.5 billion each year. Skype's software allows PC users to talk to each other for free. It also enables users to make reduced-cost calls to mobile phones and standard landline phones. At the time of the deal, Meg Whitman said, "Communications is at the heart of e-commerce and community. By combining the two leading e-commerce franchises, eBay and PayPal, with the leader in Internet voice communications, we will create an extraordinarily powerful environment for business on the net."[4]

The company is also working to strengthen its position in Asia. In 2002, eBay acquired a 33 percent share of EachNet.com, an online auction site based in Shanghai, China. This initial purchase cost eBay $30 million. It then purchased the entire company in 2004 for an additional $150 million. In 2005, eBay announced that it was investing $100 million more in EachNet.com, with the funds going toward operations. The apparent goal is for EachNet.com and eBay to dominate the online auction market in China.

EBay additionally improved its services and features for businesses that sold on the site. In 2005, the company acquired technologies from Kurant Corporation. One of these was Kurant's award-winning e-commerce software. It allowed eBay to set up a platform for small- and medium-sized businesses, as well as other sellers. This platform, called ProStores, launched in June 2005. ProStores allows eBay sellers to create their own customized virtual storefronts that operate independently from eBay.

SALES STATISTICS

In 2002, Jim Griffith shared these statistics about eBay sales:

• Someone buys a vehicle every 1.7 minutes.

• Someone buys a diamond ring every six minutes.

• A digital camera sells on the site every ninety seconds.

• People buy ten CDs and five videos every minute.

• Someone purchases a PC every thirty seconds.

• A pair of men's shoes sells every twenty-one seconds.[5]

EBay attracts all sorts of shoppers, young and old, conservatives and liberals, students and businesspeople, and on and on.

OMIDYAR LEAVES

EBay continued to grow and to prosper after the IPO, but inevitably, the company did change. As Song said, "We really lived in la-la land with our community for two wonderful years (before the IPO), and it was the time of my life. But once you go public the pressures are completely different. You've got investors and analysts looking at you, you've got the media looking at you, you've got to worry about shares and stockholders and revenue."[6]

As a result, Omidyar began to withdraw from eBay. In 2000 he decided to officially leave the company he envisioned and created, although he's still the chairman of eBay's board. The decision was not entirely unexpected. He often had expressed an interest in returning to his birth city of Paris. He and Pam also desired to have children, which can be difficult to manage with a company like eBay always demanding attention. Within a year, Pam gave birth to their daughter. They now have two children. Their stay in France did not last, however, as they decided to move to a gated community just outside of Las Vegas, Nevada. Family life now took precedence, but another matter loomed: What would Omidyar and his family do with all their money?

CHAPTER SEVEN

OMIDYAR'S PHILOSOPHY

With Omidyar's newfound wealth from the eBay IPO, he and Pam founded the Omidyar Foundation in 1998 to invest the money. Initially, the foundation invested in nonprofit organizations, which are charitable establishments that seek to benefit rather than to capitalize on society. Nonprofit organizations, however, are generally not self-sustaining financially.

Omidyar and his wife said that, over time, they became inspired by the business model they saw evolving at eBay. Omidyar, in particular, revealed that through the Web site he saw that "individuals were taking control of their own lives." He added, "They make their own lives better through their own effort . . . You can improve your community by improving your station in it . . . Businesses can help make society better."[1]

It became clear that Omidyar wanted to model his foundation on what he had created at eBay, a self-sustaining entity that was financially sound, could empower others, and would promote community building. These themes and goals have been echoed throughout his life since his days at Tufts. With them in mind, the Omidyars revamped their foundation to create the Omidyar Network in 2000. The network not only funds certain nonprofit organizations, but it also invests in profit-making companies and public policy efforts. What is particularly brilliant about the network is that money earned from the profit-making ventures goes into the nonprofit side, so, like eBay, the Omidyar Network is designed to be self-sustaining.

People and groups that the Omidyars are working with are posted on the network's Web site, http://www.omidyar.net. As of this writing, it includes the American India Foundation, which is devoted to improving social and economic conditions in India; the Apache Software Foundation, which provides computer and business support to its community; the Carter-Baker Commission, which aims to improve the United States' electoral system; the Myelin Repair Foundation, which conducts research on multiple sclerosis; Secrecy News, which aims to promote public awareness of government-held information; YouthBuild, which helps low-income youths; and several other organizations.[2]

Jeff Skoll went on to create a similar entity, the Skoll Foundation, which works with non-profit organizations from all around the globe. Skoll also has a media company called Participant Productions. It helps to produce documentaries, movies, and television shows that depict ordinary people who have made a difference in their communities. Both Omidyar and Skoll, therefore, are taking the money earned from the fees made from the sales of the CDs, jewelry, vehicles, and everything else at eBay and putting it back into society.

EBAY LIVE

In June 2005, eBay held its fourth user convention in California, eBay Live. These conventions provide eBay sellers, buyers, staff, investors, and anyone else who is interested in the company a chance to connect face to face and to hear the latest eBay news. This particular convention marked eBay's tenth anniversary. Omidyar, Skoll, Whitman, and all of the other key eBay players attended the event.

On June 23, 2005, eBay Live! was held in San Jose, California. Here, visitors are seen entering the event. On this day, the company launched a new service called ProStores. ProStores allows sellers to offer products on their own Web sites that can be searched for through eBay. The service provides sellers with the independence of having their own site while still allowing them to attract eBay's enormous membership base.

Today, eBay remains the largest, and arguably the best, online auction site. To compete with rivals, however, eBay has bought certain companies outright, such as Shopping.com, which it acquired in June 2005. To promote growth, the company also has plans to reach more potential users in various countries throughout the world. It remains to be seen how much Omidyar will contribute to these changes and to eBay's future, but it is likely that his brilliant business mind will serve as a guiding light for the company in the years to come.

OMIDYAR'S COMMENCEMENT ADDRESS

As a self-made multibillionaire who retired from the business world in his early thirties, Omidyar exemplifies everything that was, and perhaps still is, possible for entrepreneurs with a passion to turn their dreams into reality. Omidyar can speak with authority to individuals who might wish to follow in his footsteps.

In May 2002, the Omidyars gave the graduate commencement address at Tufts. During his speech, Omidyar shared what he called "a simple concept that has served me well since my time at Tufts: When you don't know what to expect . . . Prepare for the unexpected." He later added,

"To truly prepare for the unexpected, you've got to position yourself to keep a couple of options open—so when the door of opportunity opens, you're close enough to squeeze through."[3]

Omidyar and his wife, Pam, are shown here at Tufts University's 2002 graduation ceremony. On November 4, 2005, the couple donated $100 million to the school, the largest monetary gift the university had ever received. All of the money is invested in helping small-business owners in developing countries. The Omidyars hope to prove that dedicated workers can make a difference in the world, just as Pierre and Pam have done.

Omidyar exemplified the effectiveness of this strategy from an early age. Although he had planned to spend four full years at Tufts, the internship at Innovative Data Design caused him to change course because it led to a full-time position. His next job, at Claris, could have curtailed his career path because he was let go from the company. That was unexpected, since many financial analysts had predicted Claris would grow as a separate company from Apple. Omidyar kept his options open and, as a result, formed Ink Development Corporation with hopes of bringing pen-based computing into the marketplace. When that technology fizzled out, he reworked the business into eShop, a venture that made him a millionaire at the age of twenty-nine. When his hobby creation AuctionWeb began to earn him a steady income, he had to choose between quitting his stable job at General Magic and devoting all of his efforts to the auction site. Given eBay's success, it now seems accurate to say that he walked through the right door of opportunity.

Omidyar appears to make the problems that many of us struggle with, such as difficulties related to career building, seem easy to deal with.

That ease is grounded in his ability to focus on simplicity, which carried over into eBay, as he indicated during his commencement address. "By building a simple system, with just a few guiding principles," he said, "eBay was open to organic growth—it could achieve a certain degree of self-organization." He further advised, "Whatever future you're building . . . Don't try to program everything. Five Year Plans never worked for the Soviet Union," referring to the collapse of the nation in 1991. "In fact, if anything, central planning contributed to its fall."[4]

Most of all, Omidyar emphasized the importance of community, and the values that he hoped would help to govern the users and staff at eBay. The five basic values he and his wife listed reveal the principles of his work at eBay and provide some indication of what he and his family will likely promote in the future through their philanthropic ventures. "We believe people are basically good," he said. "We believe everyone has something to contribute. We believe that an honest, open environment can bring out the best in people. We recognize and respect everyone as a unique individual. We encourage you to treat others the way that you want to be treated."[5]

TIMELINE

1967— Omidyar is born in Paris, France.

1984–1988— Omidyar studies at Tufts University and finishes his education at the University of California at Berkeley.

1988–1991— Omidyar works at Innovative Data Design and Claris.

1991–1994— Omidyar cofounds Ink Development Corporation, where he serves as a software engineer.

1994–1996— Omidyar works at General Magic.

1995— Omidyar creates AuctionWeb, which later becomes eBay.

1996–1998— Omidyar serves as eBay's CEO.

1997— Benchmark Capital invests $6.5 million in eBay.

1998— Meg Whitman becomes the CEO of eBay; eBay offers stock shares to the public; Omidyar becomes a multibillionaire and co-founds the Omidyar Foundation with his wife, Pam.

TIMELINE

2000— Omidyar holds his title as chairman of eBay's board of directors, but he leaves his post at the eBay office; he co-founds the Omidyar Network with wife.

2001— Profits for eBay rise $24.6 million in just three months during an otherwise sluggish economic period.

2002— The company acquires a 33 percent stake in the Chinese auction firm EachNet.com.

2003— The San Jose headquarters of eBay is expanded.

2004— EachNet.com is purchased in full by eBay, thereby strengthening its position in Asia.

2005— The tenth anniversary of eBay is celebrated; the company holds a user's conference in San Jose, California.

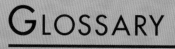

GLOSSARY

BASIC The acronym for Beginner's All-purpose Symbolic Instruction Code, which is a relatively simple computer programming language.

business-to-business (B2B) A term referring to financial deals between businesses.

business-to-consumer Retailing between a business and a consumer.

CEO Chief executive officer; the top-ranking active leader of a company.

code The system of symbols, such as numbers, letters, and punctuation marks, that make up a programming language.

e-commerce The electronic exchange of money, or something else of value, for goods and services.

headhunter Someone who helps companies to find top-notch candidates to fill open positions.

initial public offering (IPO) The process of a company offering to sell stock shares to public investors for the first time.

Internet service provider (ISP) A company that connects an individual's computer to the Internet.

libertarian A person who believes in free will and the upholding of an individual's right to have unrestricted freedom in his or her thoughts and actions.

linguistics The study of languages.

modem A device that communicates with an ISP through a computer user's phone line.

newsgroup An Internet electronic bulletin board that is dedicated to a certain topic.

nonprofit Referring to an organization that uses all of its revenues, after operating expenses are accounted for, to perform services that are meant to benefit the public.

online auction E-commerce that involves buyers and sellers who utilize bidding strategies to determine the selling prices.

semiconductor A material that affects the conductivity, or flow, of electricity and is used in the manufacture of computers.

silicon A material used as a semiconductor.

Silicon Valley A region in Northern California that is known for its computer, technology, and electronics firms.

stock Certificates that represent ownership of a corporation.

user computer A computer that enables people to access the Internet.

venture capitalist An individual or group who directly funds companies as opposed to just buying their stock.

Web browser A computer program that is used to access sites or information on a network such as the Internet.

Web server A specially designed computer that can store Web pages.

FOR MORE INFORMATION

eBay, Inc.
2145 Hamilton Avenue
San Jose, CA 95125
(408) 376-7400
e-mail: info@ebay.com
Web site: http://www.ebay.com

Maximum PC
150 North Hill Drive
Brisbane, CA 94005
(415) 468-4684
e-mail: maxcustserv@cdsfulfillment.com
Web site: http://www.maximumpc.com

Omidyar Network
1991 Broadway, Suite 200
Redwood City, CA 94063
Web site: http://www.omidyar.net

PC Magazine
Ziff Davis Media Inc.
28 East 28th Street
New York, NY 10016
e-mail: subhelp@pcmag.com
Web site: http://www.pcmag.com

PC World
PC World Communications
501 2nd Street
San Francisco, CA 94107
(415) 243-0500
Web site: http://www.pcworld.com

Skoll Foundation
250 University Avenue, Suite 200
Palo Alto, CA 94301
(650) 331-1031
Web site: http://ww.skollfoundation.org

WEB SITES

Due to the changing nature of Internet links, the Rosen Publishing Group, Inc., has developed an online list of Web sites related to the subject of this book. This site is updated regularly. Please use this link to access the list:

http://www.rosenlinks.com/icb/piom

FOR FURTHER READING

Claybourne, Anne, and Mark Wallace. *Computer Dictionary*. Tulsa, OK: EDC Publishing, 2001.

Galas, Judith. *Computers and the Internet*. Farmington Hills, MI: Thomson Gale, 2002.

Jortbert, Charles. *Mini Computers*. Edina, MN: ABDO Publishing, 1997.

Kalbag, Asha, and Russell Punter. *Computer Graphics and Animation*. Tulsa, OK: EDC Publishing, 2000.

Kalbag, Asha, and Jonathan Sheikh-Miller. *Homework on Your Computer*. Tulsa, OK: EDC Publishing, 2000.

Kaplan, Andrew, Edward Keating, and Carrie Boretz. *Careers for Computer Buffs*. Minneapolis, MN: Lerner Publishing Group, 1991.

Lesinski, Jeanne. *Bill Gates*. Minneapolis, MN: Lerner Publishing Group, 2000.

Northrup, Mary. *American Computer Pioneers*. Berkeley Heights, NJ: Enslow Publishers, 1998.

Perry, Robert L. *Personal Computer Communications*. New York, NY: Scholastic Library Publishing, 2000.

Singh, Simon. *Code Book: How to Make It, Break It, Hack It, or Crack It*. New York, NY: Bantam Doubleday Dell Books for Young Readers, 2002.

BIBLIOGRAPHY

About.com. "Hijab in French Schools." Retrieved July 2005 (http://islam.about.com/cs/ currentevents/i/france_hijab.htm).

Academy of Achievement. "Interview: Pierre Omidyar." Retrieved July 2005 (http:// www.achievement.org/autodoc/page/omi0int-1).

Cohen, Adam. *The Perfect Store: Inside eBay.* New York, NY: Little, Brown, and Company, 2002.

Gomes-Casseres, Ben. *The History of eBay.* Retrieved August 2005 (http://www.cs/brandeis.edu/ ~magnus/ief248a/eBay/history.html).

The Great Idea Finder. "Personal Computer History: Invention of the Personal Computer." Retrieved July 2005 (http://www.ideafinder.com/history/ inventions/story071.htm).

Griffith, Jim. *The Official eBay Bible.* New York, NY: Gotham Books, 2003.

How Stuff Works. "How C Programming Works." Retrieved July 2005 (http:// computer.howstuffworks.com/c.htm).

Hunter, Christopher D. "The Uses and Gratifications of Project Agora." Retrieved July (2005 http://

www.asc.upenn.edu/usr/chunter/agora_uses/
chapter_1.html).

Iran Heritage Foundation. "Dr. Elahé Mir-Djalali
Omidyar." Retrieved July 2005 (http://
www.iranheritage.org/privatelives/
bionotes_full.htm).

Kopytoff, Verne. "EBay Bids for Harmony." *San
Francisco Chronicle*, June 23, 2005.

Omidyar, Pierre, and Pam Omidyar. "From Self to
Society: Citizenship to Community for a World
of Change." Keynote address, 2002 commencement ceremony of Tufts University, Medford,
MA, May 19, 2002. Retrieved July 2005
(http://enews.tufts.edu/stories/
052002Omidyar_Pierre_keynote.htm).

Persian Mirror. "Pierre Omidyar Profile." Retrieved
July 2005 (http:// www.persianmirror.com/
culture/famous/bios/omidyar.cfm).

Richardson, John. "A Dialogue with Pierre."
Retrieved July 2005 (http://www.omidyar.net/
group/community-general/news/213/).

Stross, Randall E. *eBoys*. New York, NY: Crown
Publishers, 2000.

Tufts University. "Profile." Retrieved July 2005
(http://www.tufts.edu/home/about/?p=profile).

wsRadio.com. "Fireside Chat with eBay Founder
    Pierre Omidyar, Jeff Skoll, and Jim Griffith,
    Host of eBay Radio and Dean of Education."
    June 2005. Retrieved July 2005 (http://
    www.wsradio.com/internet-talk.cfm/radio/
    Meg-Whitman-eBay-live-key-note-speech.html).

Source Notes

Introduction

1. Jim Griffith, *The Official eBay Bible* (New York, NY: Gotham Books, 2003), p. 5.

2. Adam Cohen, *The Perfect Store: Inside eBay* (New York, NY: Little, Brown, and Company, 2002), p. 22.

3. Christopher D. Hunter, "The Uses and Gratifications of Project Agora." Retrieved July 2005 (http://www.asc.upenn.edu/usr/chunter/agora_uses/chapter_1.html).

4. Ibid.

5. John Richardson, "A Dialogue with Pierre." Retrieved July 2005 (http://www.omidyar.net/group/community-general/news/213/).

6. Silicon.com, "Gates Still World's Richest." Retrieved July 2005 (http://management.silicon.com/itdirector/0,39024673,39152747,00.htm).

Chapter 1

1. The Persian Mirror, "Pierre Omidyar Profile." Retrieved July 2005 (http://

www.persianmirror.com/culture/famous/
bios/omidyar.cfm).

2. Adam Cohen, *The Perfect Store: Inside eBay* (New York, NY: Little, Brown, and Company, 2002), p. 15.

3. About.com, "Hijab in French Schools." Retrieved July 2005 (http://islam.about.com/cs/currentevents/i/france_hijab.htm).

4. Iran Heritage Foundation, "Dr. Elahé Mir-Djalali Omidyar." Retrieved July 2005 (http://www.iranheritage.org/privatelives/bionotes_full.htm).

5. Academy of Achievement, "Interview: Pierre Omidyar." Retrieved July 2005 (http://www.achievement.org/autodoc/page/omi0int-1).

6. Ibid.

7. Ibid.

8. Ibid.

9. Ibid.

10. Cohen, p. 16.

11. Academy of Achievement, "Interview: Pierre Omidyar."

12. Ibid.

13. Ibid.

Chapter 2

1. Academy of Achievement. "Interview: Pierre Omidyar." Retrieved July 2005 (http://www.achievement.org/autodoc/page/omi0int-1).

2. Tufts University, "Profile." Retrieved July 2005 (http://www.tufts.edu/home/about/?p=profile).

3. Ibid.

4. Ibid.

5. Ibid.

6. Academy of Achievement, "Interview: Pierre Omidyar."

7. Academy of Achievement, "Interview: Pierre Omidyar."

8. The Great Idea Finder, "Personal Computer History: Invention of the Personal Computer." Retrieved July 2005 (http://www.ideafinder.com/history/inventions/story071.htm).

9. Adam Cohen, *The Perfect Store: Inside eBay* (New York, NY: Little, Brown, and Company, 2002), p. 16.

CHAPTER 3

1. Academy of Achievement, "Interview: Pierre Omidyar." Retrieved July 2005 (http://www.achievement.org/autodoc/page/omi0int-1).

2. Adam Cohen, *The Perfect Store: Inside eBay* (New York, NY: Little, Brown, and Company, 2002), p. 24.

3. Ibid., p. 25.

4. Ibid., p. 29.

5. Ibid., pp. 27–28.

CHAPTER 4

1. Adam Cohen, *The Perfect Store: Inside eBay* (New York, NY: Little, Brown, and Company, 2002), p. 21.

2. Ibid., p. 35.

3. Randall E. Stross, *eBoys* (New York, NY: Crown Publishers, 2000), p. 24.

CHAPTER 5

1. U.S. Department of Transportation, "U.S. Major Airlines Report Another Stellar Year of Operating and Net Profits in 1998." May 9, 1999. Retrieved

July 2005 (http://www.dot.gov/affairs/1999/dot6599.htm).

2. Adam Cohen, *The Perfect Store* (New York, NY: Little, Brown, and Company, 2002), p. 46.

3. Ibid., p. 55.

4. Ibid., p. 93.

5. Ibid., p. 82.

6. Ibid., p. 83.

7. Ibid., p. 308.

CHAPTER 6

1. Adam Cohen, *The Perfect Store: Inside eBay* (New York, NY: Little, Brown, and Company, 2002), p. 110.

2. wsRadio.com, "Fireside Chat with eBay Founder Pierre Omidyar, Jeff Skoll, and Jim Griffith, Host of eBay Radio and Dean of Education." Retrieved July 2005 (http://www.wsradio.com/internet-talk.cfm/radio/Meg-Whitman-eBay-live-key-note-speech.html)

3. Cohen, p. 148.

4. BBC News, "EBay to buy Skype in $2.6bn deal." Retrieved February 21, 2006 (http://news.bbc.co.uk/1/hi/business/4237338.stm).

5. Jim Griffith, *The Official eBay Bible* (New York, NY: Gotham Books, 2003), p. 7.

6. Cohen, p.305.

CHAPTER 7

1. wsRadio.com, "Fireside Chat with eBay Founder Pierre Omidyar, Jeff Skoll, and Jim Griffith, Host of eBay Radio and Dean of Education." Retrieved July 2005 (http://www.wsradio.com/ internet-talk.cfm/radio/Meg-Whitman-eBay- live-key-note-speech.html).

2. The Omidyar Network, "Network Partners." Retrieved August 2005 (http://www.omidyar.net/ corp/partners.shtml).

3. Pierre Omidyar and Pam Omidyar, "From Self to Society: Citizenship to Community for a World of Change" (keynote address, Tufts University, Medford, MA, May 19, 2002). Retrieved July 2005 (http://enews.tufts.edu/stories/ 052002Omidyar_Pierre_keynote.htm).

4. Ibid.

5. Ibid.

INDEX

ABOUT THE AUTHOR

Jennifer Viegas is a news reporter for the Discovery Channel, Animal Planet, the Travel Channel, TLC, and the Australian Broadcasting Corporation. At eBay, she has bought everything from a 1949 set of New York Yankees baseball cards to an autographed CD of singer Lana Cantrell that was sold to her by Cantrell herself.

PHOTO CREDITS

Cover, p. 3 (portrait) © Kim Kulish/Corbis; cover and p. 3 Web page adapted from www.ebay.com; cover and interior pages background graphic © Royalty-Free/Corbis; p. 6 © Nathaniel Welch/Corbis; p. 10 © Ed Kashi/Corbis; p. 12 © James D. Wilson/ Liaison Agency/Getty Images; p. 15 © Charles E. Rotkin/Corbis; p. 21 © SSPL/The Image Works; p. 25 Digital Collections and Archives, Tufts University; p. 30 © Ralph Morse/Time Life Pictures/ Getty Images; p. 31 image © Andy Warhol Foundation/Corbis, artwork © The Andy Warhol Foundation for the Visual Arts/ Corbis; p. 36 © RNT Productions/Corbis; pp. 38, 45, 51, 55 from eBay Workshop, eBay History 101; pp. 40, 63, 67, 77, 87 © AP/Wide World Photos; p. 47 © Bob Daemmrich/The Image Works; p. 59 © John Harding/ Time Life Pictures/Getty Images; p. 69 © Tim Chapman/Getty Images; p. 71 © Kevin Horan/Time Life Pictures/Getty Images; p. 80 © Alex Farnsworth/The Image Works; p. 82 © Tom & Dee Ann McCarthy/Corbis; p. 89 © Mark Morrelli for Tufts University.

Designer: Nelson Sá; Editor: Nicholas Croce
Photo Researcher: Jeffrey Wendt

DATE DUE